Arctic Ocean

30°E 60° 90° 120° 150°

EUROPE

ASIA

ISRAEL

AFRICA

Pacific

Ocean

Indian

Ocean

AUSTRALIA

ANTARCTICA

Israel

Emma Young

Zvi Ben-Dor Benite, George Kanazi, and Aviva Halamish, Consultants

NATIONAL GEOGRAPHIC

WASHINGTON, D.C.

Contents

Foreword

srael is a Jewish state. It was established in 1948 by and for Jews returning to their historic homeland after living in exile for thousands of years. In Israel, you can meet people from all corners of the world who speak dozens of languages, building a new life and a common future, while still preserving their particular traditions and customs. Israel is also the state of its Arab citizens. They have been living here for hundreds of years and constitute about one fifth of the population.

Israel is a young democracy—it is only 60 years old. It is a modern Western-oriented state situated in a very ancient land. Here you can follow in the footsteps of Biblical figures, visit archeological excavations, and get a real sense of how people lived many years ago—Jews, Christians, Muslims, and others. Yet you will also find modern industrial, scientific, and agricultural enterprises here, as well as social experiments like communal life on a type of farm that only exists in Israel, the kibbutz.

Israel constitutes a unique geographical entity. Where else in the world can you find a country so tiny in area with such a diversity of landscapes, climates, flora, fauna, and people? When it is cold and snowy up in the mountains, half an hour's drive will bring you to the lowest point on Earth, where you can swim in the warm Dead Sea.

As the birthplace of many different civilizations and religions, Israel, and especially its capital, Jerusalem, is sacred to millions of people around the world. But the country has long been afflicted by conflict and violence. Unfortunately, it is still the object of bitter rivalry between faiths and peoples.

I hope you will enjoy the fascinating journey that this book takes you on through Israel's past and present. You will meet a vibrant society. It is burdened by its past, but it is also looking forward to a better future for all the inhabitants of this beautiful and beloved land.

▲ Ethiopian Jews study
Hebrew after arriving in
Israel. Immigration
is responsible for most
population growth
in Israel.

Aviva Halamish
The Open University of Israel

A *Promised Land*

ACCORDING TO THE BIBLE, the Hebrews—the ancestors of today's Jewish Israelis—arrived in what is now Israel after traveling for many years through a dry wilderness. God had promised that they would reach a land that was "flowing with milk and honey." In fact, it took a lot of work to make Israel fertile. In the south, much of the land is still too dry to be farmed.

Israelis are very proud of turning empty areas into farmland by draining marshes or pumping river water to desert areas. In the process, Israel has become a world leader in advanced farming techniques. Where the Bible says the Hebrews once wandered through a desert, green fields are now watered using computer technology and greenhouse plants grow without soil.

◀ The Wilderness of Zin lies at the heart of the Negev Desert in southern Israel. This mountainous area of desert is largely unchanged since the time of Moses.

WHAT'S THE WEATHER LIKE?

The drive from the north of Israel to the farthest point south only takes about six hours—but it covers a huge variation in climate. In winter, people ski down mountain slopes in the north. To the south, the climate is milder and there is frequent rain along the west coast. In the east, it is warm enough to swim in the Dead Sea on most days of the year.

The climate is very dry farther south. The southern tip of the Negev Desert receives just 1 inch (32mm) of rain a year. In summer, desert temperatures soar to above 104°F (40°C), while the coastal area becomes humid and sunny.

Labels on this map and on similar maps throughout this book identify most of the places pictured in each chapter.

Fast Facts

OFFICIAL NAME: State of Israel

FORM OF GOVERNMENT: Parliamentary Democracy

CAPITAL: Jerusalem

POPULATION: 7,171,600

OFFICIAL LANGUAGES: Hebrew, Arabic

MONETARY UNIT: shekel

AREA: 7,886 square miles (20,325 square kilometers)

BORDERING NATIONS: Egypt, Jordan, Lebanon, Palestinian Authority, Syria

HIGHEST POINT: Mount Meron (Har Meron) 3,963 feet (1,208 meters)

LOWEST POINT: Dead Sea, 1,365 feet (416 meters) below sea level

MAJOR LAKES: Sea of Galilee, Dead Sea

MAJOR RIVER: Jordan

0	50 mi
0	50 km

Mediterranean Sea

MAP KEY
Mild
- Mediterranean
Dry
- Arid

Average Temperature & Rainfall

Average High/Low Temperatures; Yearly Rainfall

HAIFA (NORTH COAST)
88° F (31° C) / 48° F (9° C); 21 in (54 cm)

TEL AVIV (CENTRAL COAST)
86° F (30° C) / 50° F (10° C); 21 in (52 cm)

JERUSALEM (CENTRAL)
84° F (29° C) / 43° F (6° C); 22 in (55 cm)

ELAT (SOUTH)
104° F (40° C) / 50° F (10° C); 1 in (3 cm)

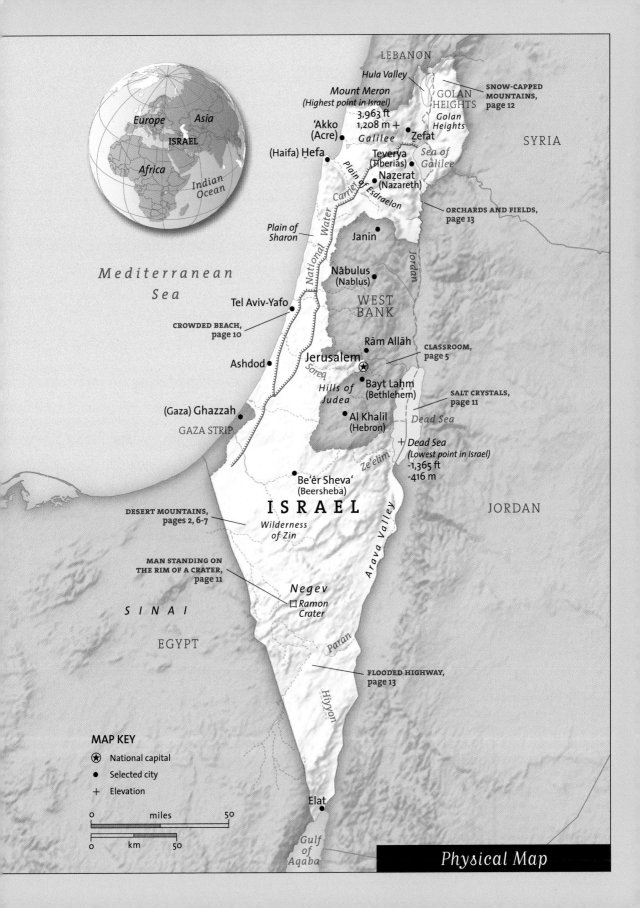

LEBANON

Hula Valley

GOLAN
HEIGHTS

SNOW-CAPPED
MOUNTAINS,
page 12

Mount Meron
(Highest point in Israel)
3,963 ft
1,208 m +

Golan
Heights

'Akko
(Acre)

Galilee

Zefat

SYRIA

(Haifa) Ḥefa

Teverya
(Tiberias)

Sea of
Galilee

Nazerat
(Nazareth)

ORCHARDS AND FIELDS,
page 13

Plain of
Esdraelon

Plain of
Sharon

Janin

Jordan

Mediterranean
Sea

Nābulus
(Nablus)

WEST
BANK

Tel Aviv-Yafo

CROWDED BEACH,
page 10

Rām Allāh

CLASSROOM,
page 5

Jerusalem

Ashdod

Soreq

Bayt Laḥm
(Bethlehem)

SALT CRYSTALS,
page 11

Hills of
Judea

Al Khalil
(Hebron)

Dead Sea

(Gaza) Ghazzah

GAZA STRIP

Ze'elim

+ *Dead Sea*
(Lowest point in Israel)
-1,365 ft
-416 m

JORDAN

Be'ér Sheva'
(Beersheba)

ISRAEL

DESERT MOUNTAINS,
pages 2, 6-7

Wilderness
of Zin

Arava Valley

MAN STANDING ON
THE RIM OF A CRATER,
page 11

Negev

□ *Ramon*
Crater

S I N A I

EGYPT

Paran

FLOODED HIGHWAY,
page 13

Ḥiyyon

MAP KEY

⊛ National capital

● Selected city

+ Elevation

o ___ miles ___ 50

o ___ km ___ 50

Elat

Gulf
of
Aqaba

Physical Map

Europe   Asia

ISRAEL

Africa

Indian
Ocean

Little Country, Big Player

Israel is a sliver of land about the size of New Jersey—but it has a huge importance throughout the world because of its history and location. It is a new country, created only in the late 1940s, but its ancient past is sacred for three of the world's major religions: Judaism, Christianity, and Islam. It is also an important crossroads at the heart of the Middle East, where Europe, Asia, and Africa meet.

Hills and Valleys

Although Israel is small, it contains many landscapes: green valleys, snowy mountains, rocky deserts, and golden beaches. A range of mountains and hills runs down the center of the country. More than half of all Israelis live west of the highlands, on the narrow coastal plain beside the Mediterranean Sea.

In the north of Israel, Galilee is a plateau—a high, flat area—that has the country's best farmland. South of Galilee the Jerzeel Valley is a fertile region that produces grapes and

▲ You are never far from the sea in Israel. The beaches of Tel Aviv are often crowded.

▶ Olives are one of Israel's most important food crops. They are eaten whole and pressed to make oil.

DESERT CRATER

The Negev Desert in southern Israel contains the huge Ramon Crater. Unlike other craters, this huge hole in the ground was not caused by a meteorite colliding with Earth. Instead the crater was created when a hill was gradually worn away by rain over millions of years. The heart-shaped hole is 25 miles (40 km) long and 1,640 feet (500 meters) deep at its lowest point. The crater is now a refuge for desert wildlife and an important geological center. The cliffs of its sides expose layers of rocks. The oldest layers are 200 million years old.

▲ The Ramon Crater is named after the Arabic word for "Roman." It was once on the Roman trade route between Egypt and the Middle East.

olives. In ancient times, the valley formed the route between two great centers of civilization: Egypt and Mesopotamia. On the other side of the wide valley, the land rises to the Judean Hills, which contain Jerusalem, the Israeli capital. Rainfall is heavier in the hills than elsewhere, and in winter Jerusalem is sometimes covered in a thin layer of snow.

Scorching South

The southern half of Israel is made up of the Negev region. Although the hills of the north receive just enough water for farming, the south is a rocky desert. Underwater springs create a few oases, or small fertile areas where plants can grow.

▼ Large blocks of salt crystals poke above the shallow water of the Dead Sea.

▲ The top of Mount Hermon—a peak in the Golan Heights, part of Syria controlled by Israel, is covered in snow. The melting snow provides most of the water in the Sea of Galilee and the Jordan River.

The Negev meets the Red Sea at Elat, Israel's gateway to shipping routes to Asia.

Some of Israel's eastern border is formed by the Jordan Valley. This huge valley marks the place where two of the plates that make up Earth's surface meet. In the south, the valley contains the Dead Sea, the lowest point on Earth. The sea, which is actually a lake, lies 1,365 feet (416 m) below sea level on the border of Israel and Jordan. The sea is fed by Israel's main river, the Jordan, but it has nowhere water can drain out. Instead, water evaporates in the heat. Minerals get concentrated in the water that is left. They make the Dead Sea the world's saltiest sea— no plants or fish can live there.

South of the Dead Sea is a dry grassland called the Arava. During the summer the Arava and Negev are hit by scorching desert winds called *khamsin*, or *sharav* in Hebrew. The winds blow east from the deserts of Arabia for up to five days at a time. They can destroy crops and cover everything in sand and dust.

A Holy Watering Place

Before it reaches the Dead Sea, the Jordan River feeds the Sea of Galilee, the main source of Israel's fresh

DELUGE!

Thunderstorms in the Negev sometimes bring disastrous floods. If clouds above the desert suddenly cool and the wind drops, all the rain falls onto a small area and can cause catastrophe. Almost one inch (2.5 cm) of rain can fall within a few minutes.

The Dead Sea area is also prone to flash flooding because it is located so far below sea level. The water cannot escape anywhere. Spring rain from Jerusalem and the surrounding hills rushes down to the sea through steep valleys. The water forms raging torrents that often rip up trees, wreck crops, and block highways, leaving travelers stranded.

▲ Water floods across a road in the Negev Desert, stopping vehicles in their tracks.

water. The river was once a major waterway, but today it is often only a trickle. Sometimes, experts say, it is only used water running back in from farms and factories that keeps the river flowing. Israel and its neighbor, Jordan, take 90 percent of the river's water to use for drinking, industry, or irrigation. The region is so dry, and water is so valuable, that neither side wants to give up their rights to the Jordan River. In Israel, a system of canals and pipes diverts water into once-dry areas. It allows a large area, including the Negev, to be used for farming.

▼ The Jordan River takes a winding course through eastern Israel, providing water for orchards and fields.

The Desert Searcher

AS NIGHT FALLS, ISRAEL'S striped hyenas get ready to leave their family dens. The young stay at home surrounded by the bones of recent meals. The hyenas are equipped with sharp teeth and long claws, but they are not killers. Instead they search the Negev Desert scavenging for the remains of dead animals.

Each hyena searches alone, sniffing out dead bodies with its sensitive nose. When it finds some food, its wide jaws are strong enough to crack into bones to get at the tasty and nutritious bone marrow inside. The powerful teeth are effective weapons— producing one of the strongest bites in the animal kingdom. To warn off attackers, the hyena raises the hairs of its neck, which makes it appear much larger.

◀ A hyena pup with its mother at a den in the Negev Desert. Although hyenas are often thought of as doglike animals, they are more closely related to cats.

SAVING WILDLIFE

Shooting wild animals was a popular sport in West Asia in the 19th century. As a result, cheetahs, Nile crocodiles, and Syrian brown bears vanished from what is now Israel. In the desert some more unusual animals also disappeared, such as the onager (a wild ass) and the Arabian oryx (a type of antelope). As these animals vanished, large predators such as wolves had less to eat, and so their numbers also fell.

Since the 1960s Israel has taken several steps to save endangered species. Nature reserves now cover 20 percent of the land, protecting ostriches, wolves, foxes, leopards, hyenas, snakes, and lizards.

Much of what is now Israel was originally covered in woodland. By the early 20th century, much of this had been cut down for timber and to make way for fields. Despite the growth in Israel's population in the last 50 years and the resulting increase in the area of farmland in the country, woodlands are being replanted in all available places.

Species at Risk

A few Israeli reserves aim to breed threatened species of birds and animals, and to re-introduce some that have died out in the wild. The captive animals learn to survive alone in special pens before they are released into the wild. Onagers, Arabian oryxes, fallow deer, and vultures have already returned to Israel's landscape as a result.

Species at risk include:
> African skimmer (bird)
> Arouss Al Ayn (salamander)
> Atlantic petrel (bird)
> Audouin's gull
> Audubon's shearwater (bird)
> Bateleur (bird)
> Black-tailed godwit (bird)
> Cinereous vulture
> Corncrake (bird)
> Dalmatian pelican
> Ferruginous duck
> Giant devilray (fish)
> Great snipe (bird)
> Pallid harrier (bird)
> Piked dogfish
> Red-breasted goose
> Rock hyrax
> Short-toed snake eagle
> Smalltooth sawfish
> Sociable lapwing (bird)

▲ Two baby hyraxes rest on their mother's back in a shady crevice in Galilee. Hyraxes might not look it, but they are the closest living relatives to elephants.

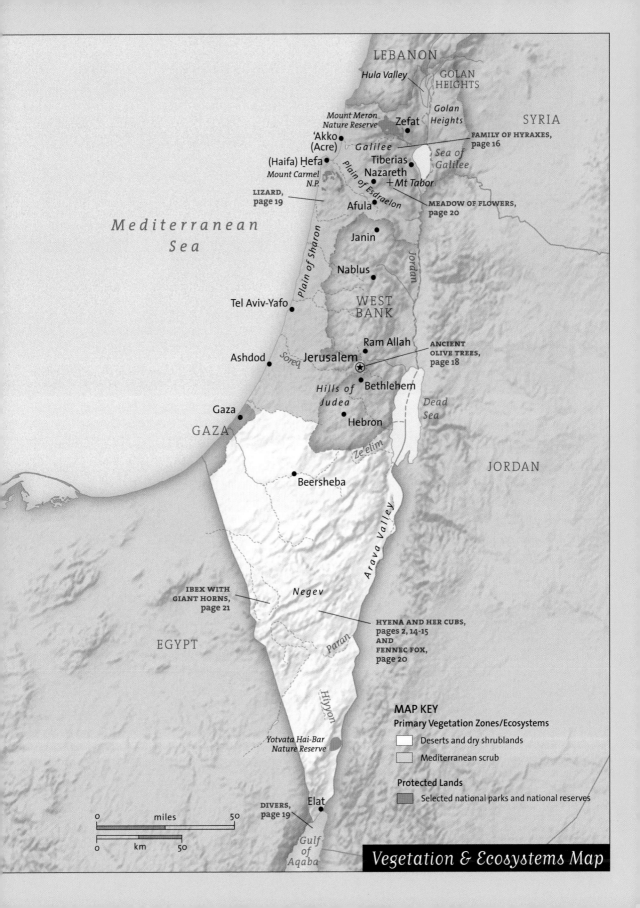

LEBANON

Hula Valley

GOLAN
HEIGHTS

*Golan
Heights*

SYRIA

*Mount Meron
Nature Reserve* Zefat

'Akko
(Acre) *Galilee*

*Sea of
Galilee*

FAMILY OF HYRAXES,
page 16

(Haifa) Ḥefa Tiberias
Nazareth

*Mount Carmel
N.P.* +Mt Tabor

LIZARD,
page 19

Plain of Esdraelon

MEADOW OF FLOWERS,
page 20

Afula

*Mediterranean
Sea*

Janin

Nablus

Plain of Sharon

Tel Aviv-Yafo

WEST
BANK

Ram Allah

ANCIENT
OLIVE TREES,
page 18

Ashdod

Soreq

Jerusalem
★

Bethlehem

*Hills of
Judea*

*Dead
Sea*

Gaza

GAZA

Hebron

JORDAN

Ze'elim

Beersheba

Arava Valley

IBEX WITH
GIANT HORNS,
page 21

Negev

HYENA AND HER CUBS,
pages 2, 14-15
AND
FENNEC FOX,
page 20

EGYPT

Paran

Hiyyon

MAP KEY

Primary Vegetation Zones/Ecosystems

Deserts and dry shrublands

Mediterranean scrub

*Yotvata Hai-Bar
Nature Reserve*

Protected Lands

Selected national parks and national reserves

DIVERS,
page 19

Elat

0   miles   50

0   km   50

*Gulf
of
Aqaba*

Vegetation & Ecosystems Map

▲ Ancient olive trees grow in the Garden of Gethsemane in Jerusalem, where according to Christian tradition, Jesus Christ was arrested before being crucified. Olive groves cover many of the hills in Israel and the West Bank.

A Living Menagerie

Because of Israel's variety of terrain and climate, the country has a large number of different animals crammed into its small area. Boars roam the damp oak woodlands of the Golan Heights. Caspian turtles live in marshlands along the coast. Lizards crawl over rocks and walls even in the heart of big cities. Fruit bats flit around the trees in city parks. Snakes sometimes slither through gardens. Most are harmless, but Israeli children learn to be careful when turning over rocks.

Home and Away

Israel's skies are a busy place in spring and fall. The country lies on the main migration routes used by birds flying between Europe, Asia, and Africa.

An estimated 1.5 billion birds fly over the land twice a year. Honey buzzards, storks, and pelicans are among these travelers. Aircraft are kept away from the birds' main paths.

At dawn during spring, tens of thousands of birds stop off at the salt flats north of Elat. Having flown across 2,000 miles (3,219 km) of desert they need a meal. Juicy plants growing on the flats called seablite provide them with exactly that.

Underwater Jungle

A stunning coral reef stretches about 3,900 feet (1,200 meters) along the Elat shore. The reef's huge structure looks like rock, but is actually covered in colonies of tiny animals called coral polyps. As the polyps die, their remains build up over millions of years to form mounds of limestone.

The reef is home to much more than colorful corals. Crabs, sea anemones, turtles, sea urchins, cuttlefish, moray eels, and octopuses are commonly seen around the reef. Sharks and dolphins also visit regularly.

Rare hawksbill turtles nest on Elat's beaches. They bury their eggs in the sand before

ARMORED LIZARD

The star agama, or hardun, is the largest lizard in Israel. Agamas up to 12 inches (30 cm) long can be seen basking in the sunshine on rocks and trees throughout the country. The agama's scales are spiny, especially around the neck. Agamas eat insects, small lizards, and flowers.

▼ The agama can change the color of its skin: It gets slightly darker when it is cold.

▼ The waters along Israel's narrow sliver of Red Sea coast contain some spectacular corals and other colorful sea creatures.

NORTHERN TERRITORY

Galilee in northern Israel has its own distinct climate and natural life. It is a hilly plateau that is colder and wetter than the rest of Israel. As a result, its lush landscape is riddled with streams and waterfalls and is home to a great variety of wildflowers, such as tulips, lupines, and honeysuckle. In spring the hillsides turn pink, white, and yellow as the flowers bloom. Galilee is also home to animals such as mountain gazelles, rock hyraxes, and cranes.

▼ Red poppies carpet the ground near Mount Tabor in southern Galilee.

▼ A fennec fox's large ears allow it to locate prey in the dark by sound alone.

returning to the sea. When the eggs hatch 60 days later, the hatchlings must scurry to the sea before predators, like crabs and gulls, catch them.

Desert Survival

In the dry areas of the Arava and the Negev, plants must be able to survive without much water and withstand large amounts of salt. They are often long-rooted, bringing water up from far below the surface, and have few leaves, so that they do not lose water very quickly. One such plant is gypsophila, also known as Baby's Breath, used around the world to decorate bouquets of flowers. The red lotus has a different way of surviving the heat. It has a layer of hairs that stops the wind from drying out the plant.

Animals have adapted to the desert, too. The fennec fox is the world's smallest dog. Its enormous ears help to rid its body of heat. When water is scarce, it can survive on the moisture in its food.

Desert trees, such as acacias, provide leafy food for occasional gazelles and the ibex, a kind of wild goat. Date palms grow around desert oases.

Going Green

Over the last 60 years more than 200 million trees have been planted in Israel. Most are pine trees, which grow in wet and dry conditions and so can be found more or less all over the country. Oaks, dramatic-looking pistachios, and cypress trees grow in the cooler north and western areas.

In the 1960s a campaign began to discourage people from picking wildflowers to keep Israel's countryside beautiful. In December, hyacinth, narcissus, and crocus cover the mountain slopes. The almond trees blossom in spring. The central forests and northern Negev are covered with anemones and cyclamens. Orchids bloom on the hillsides of Jerusalem.

▼ An old male ibex has huge horns. Few other males would challenge him, as they could not defeat him in a fight.

The *Holy Land*

JERUSALEM IS NO ORDINARY city. For 5,000 years, it has been at the heart of history. Jerusalem is an important place not just for the people who live there, but also for billions of Jews, Muslims, and Christians all over the world. For Christians, the Church of the Holy Sepulcher in the Old City marks the place where Jesus Christ was crucified and rose from the dead. According to Muslims, the shrine on the Temple Mount is the place from which Muhammad ascended to heaven. In Jewish tradition, meanwhile, Jerusalem is where the Messiah will one day appear. The three religions have long fought over the Holy City and the rest of Israel's ancient land. The country is still dominated by a struggle for ownership between Jews and Arabs.

◀ Jews pray at the Western Wall in Jerusalem, their most sacred shrine. The golden Dome of the Rock on the Temple Mount above is Islam's third most holy site.

ANCIENT CIVILIZATIONS

In Israel, even the most ancient history is vital to modern life. People look to the past for evidence of who should own the land today.

At 9,500 years old, the Arab city of Jericho is one of the world's oldest settlements. The ancient site contains some of the first evidence anywhere that people had learned how to farm crops and animals.

Little is known about the earliest inhabitants of modern Israel. After about 2000 B.C. it was home to the Canaanites, who were later overthrown by the Israelites. Other powers also dominated the area at different times in its history: Egyptians, Babylonians, Persians, Greeks, Romans, and Islamic rulers. Each conqueror left a mark, and the fighting still goes on.

▲ **These tombs in the Negev Desert are about 6,000 years old. They were built by people living along the trade route that connected ancient civilizations in Turkey, Iraq, and Egypt.**

Time line

This chart shows the approximate dates of events in the history of the Jewish people and the different rulers of the land that is now the State of Israel.

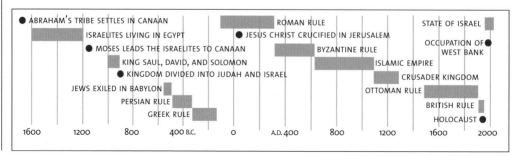

- ABRAHAM'S TRIBE SETTLES IN CANAAN
- ISRAELITES LIVING IN EGYPT
- MOSES LEADS THE ISRAELITES TO CANAAN
- KING SAUL, DAVID, AND SOLOMON
- KINGDOM DIVIDED INTO JUDAH AND ISRAEL
- JEWS EXILED IN BABYLON
- PERSIAN RULE
- GREEK RULE
- ROMAN RULE
- JESUS CHRIST CRUCIFIED IN JERUSALEM
- BYZANTINE RULE
- ISLAMIC EMPIRE
- OTTOMAN RULE
- STATE OF ISRAEL
- OCCUPATION OF WEST BANK
- CRUSADER KINGDOM
- BRITISH RULE
- HOLOCAUST

1600   1200   800   400 B.C.   0   A.D. 400   800   1200   1600   2000

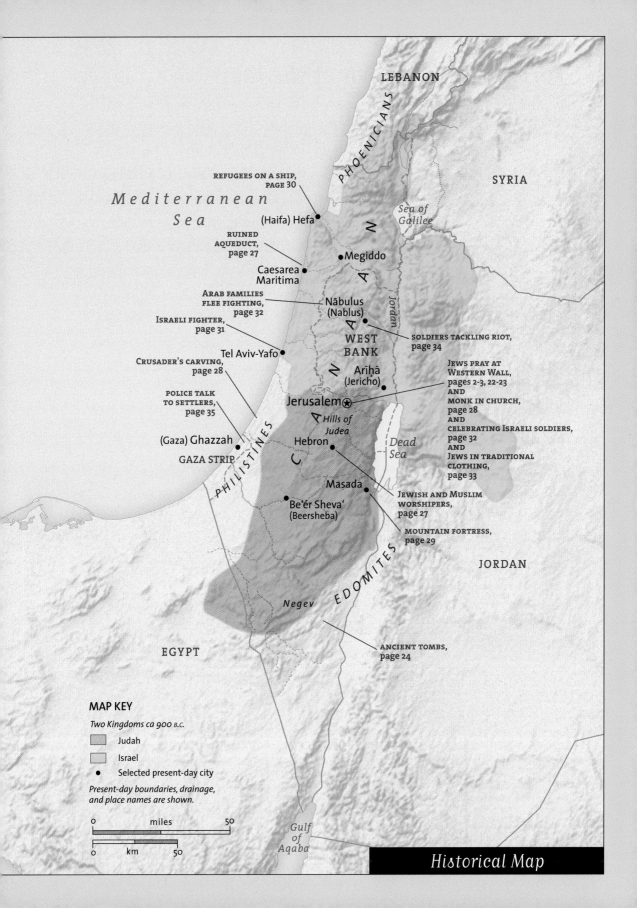

LEBANON

*Mediterranean
Sea*

REFUGEES ON A SHIP,
PAGE 30

(Haifa) Hefa

RUINED
AQUEDUCT,
page 27

Caesarea
Maritima

ARAB FAMILIES
FLEE FIGHTING,
page 32

ISRAELI FIGHTER,
page 31

Tel Aviv-Yafo

CRUSADER'S CARVING,
page 28

POLICE TALK
TO SETTLERS,
page 35

(Gaza) Ghazzah

GAZA STRIP

PHOENICIANS

SYRIA

*Sea of
Galilee*

Megiddo

C A N A A N

Nābulus
(Nablus)

WEST
BANK

Jordan

SOLDIERS TACKLING RIOT,
page 34

Arīḥā
(Jericho)

Jerusalem

*Hills of
Judea*

Hebron

*Dead
Sea*

C A N A A N

P H I L I S T I N E S

Masada

Be'ér Sheva'
(Beersheba)

JEWS PRAY AT
WESTERN WALL,
pages 2-3, 22-23
AND
MONK IN CHURCH,
page 28
AND
CELEBRATING ISRAELI SOLDIERS,
page 32
AND
JEWS IN TRADITIONAL
CLOTHING,
page 33

JEWISH AND MUSLIM
WORSHIPERS,
page 27

MOUNTAIN FORTRESS,
page 29

JORDAN

Negev

E D O M I T E S

EGYPT

ANCIENT TOMBS,
page 24

*Gulf
of
Aqaba*

MAP KEY

Two Kingdoms ca 900 B.C.

Judah

Israel

• Selected present-day city

*Present-day boundaries, drainage,
and place names are shown.*

0   miles   50

0   km   50

Historical Map

The Birth of the Jews

The story of modern Israel begins more than 3,500 years ago. Most Israelis are Jews, who are said to be descended from the biblical figure Abraham, through his son Isaac. They were originally a group of tribes known as Israelites. Abraham led the Israelites from Mesopotamia (now Iraq) to the Judean Hills of what was then called Canaan. However, a famine later forced them to move to Egypt before Moses led them back in 1250 B.C. According to Jewish and Christian belief, God promised the land of Israel to the descendants of Abraham, Isaac, and Isaac's son, Jacob. For many people, such a promise is like many other Bible stories: It may not be the literal truth. For many other people, however, that promise is one of the central foundations of the nation of Israel.

▲ In the Bible, the future King David killed Goliath, a giant Philistine warrior, with just a single sling shot. A sling is a weapon made from cloth and string that fires stones. David's victory marked the turning point in the Israelites' struggle to control the land that became Israel.

The Promised Land

The returning Israelites fought for 200 years for control of Canaan. Their main enemies were the Philistines, a powerful tribe from Crete that settled along the southern coast. (The modern name for the Arabs living in the region comes from the word *Philistine*: Palestinian.) In 1006 B.C., King Saul united the Israelite tribes but was defeated by the Philistines and killed himself.

Saul's son-in-law, David, eventually overcame the Philistines and conquered Jerusalem. David's son, King Solomon, is famous for building the Temple at

Jerusalem. It became the center of the Jewish religion.

Changing Rulers

Following Solomon's death, the Israelites split into two small kingdoms. One, called Israel, was in the north of what is now Galilee and the West Bank. (The West Bank is an area of Jordan that is occupied by Israel.) The second kingdom, called Judah, was centered on the city of Jerusalem.

Israel became part of the Assyrian Empire in 722 B.C. and Judah was conquered by Babylonians in 586 B.C. The Temple in Jerusalem was destroyed and the people of Judah taken into captivity in Babylon (in

▲ The remains of an aqueduct at Caesarea Maritima, which was a port built by the Romans in 13 B.C. on Israel's northern coast.

FAMILY TIES

Although Arabs—who are mainly Muslims—and Jews are bitterly divided by politics, their respective faiths actually share a number of elements. Both groups claim descent from the same ancestor: the prophet Abraham.

Jews see themselves as the children of Abraham's second son Isaac. However, according to Islam, Abraham's oldest son, Ishmael, is the central figure. Ishmael is believed to be buried in a tomb at the holiest Muslim shrine at Mecca. Abraham is buried in Hebron in the West Bank. His tomb is sacred for both religions and both claim the land around it as their own.

▲ A Jewish rabbi and a Muslim cleric pray to their respective gods at Abraham's tomb.

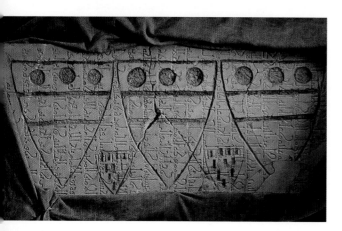

today's Iraq). Forty years later, the Persians conquered Babylonia and allowed the Jews to return home. In Jerusalem, the Jews rebuilt the Temple of Solomon. In the fourth century B.C., however, the Jews were again conquered. Alexander the Great began a period of Greek control in which rulers tried to outlaw the Jewish faith.

In 63 B.C. the region became part of the Roman Empire. Over the years the Jews had divided into several groups, but they united to revolt against the Romans in A.D. 66. The Romans crushed the rebellion and destroyed Jerusalem. Only the western wall of the Temple survived. The Romans drove the Jews out of Jerusalem. Many were sold into slavery or left their homeland altogether.

▲ The Church of the Holy Sepulcher in Jerusalem contains the site of Christ's tomb.

▼ An English knight carved his coat of arms over this Arabic writing after the Crusaders took control of the Holy Land from its Muslim rulers.

Muslims and Crusaders

In A.D. 638, only two decades after a new religion called Islam had originated in Arabia, an Arab army captured Jerusalem. According to Muslim tradition (Muslims are followers of Islam), the Prophet Muhammad had risen to heaven from a rock on top of the Temple Mount to be given his instructions by God. Muslims ruled what is now Israel for almost 1,300 years.

MOUNTAIN FORTRESS

In A.D. 66, the Jews rebelled against Roman rule. The Romans crushed the rebels quickly, but one stronghold, Masada, was able to hold out until A.D. 73. The fortress, located in the desert close to the Dead Sea, was in the hands of Zealots (religious rebel fighters). Rather than surrender to the Romans laying siege to Masada, the 1,000 Jewish defenders chose to commit mass suicide.

▶ Masada is a flat-topped mountain. Today, Israeli soldiers are sworn in on its summit.

At first, the new rulers were more tolerant than the Greeks and Romans had been. They allowed both Jews and Christians to practice their faiths. However, in the late 10th century the caliph, the leader of the Islamic Empire, called for Muslims to pull down the churches in Jerusalem. In response, Pope Urban II, head of the Christian Roman Catholic church, called for Jerusalem and the rest of the "Holy Land" to be brought under Christian rule. In 1099 an army of Europeans, known as Crusaders, invaded and set up a series of small states. A series of Christian invasions—known as the Crusades—continued until 1270, when Muslims overthrew the last of the Crusader States.

A Home for the Jews?

A more peaceful time began in 1517, when the region became a quiet corner of the huge Turkish Ottoman Empire. After World War I (1914–1918) that empire collapsed. The peace treaties at the end of the war gave the British temporary control of what was known at the time as Palestine.

Jews in Palestine and elsewhere saw a chance to create a Jewish homeland after many centuries of foreign rule or exile. Meanwhile, most people in Palestine were Arabs whose ancestors had lived there for over a thousand years. They also wanted an independent state. The British agreed to let Jews build up their communities in Palestine, but also promised to protect the rights of Palestinian Arabs.

When Adolf Hitler's Nazi Party took power in Germany in 1933, many Jews left to escape their

ZIONISM

▲ Jewish survivors of the Holocaust arrive in Haifa by ship in 1946 hoping to build a new life.

In the 19th century only a few thousand Jews were left in the land that is now Israel. For centuries most had lived in Europe where they were often persecuted. This got worse in Russia in the 1880s with mass killings of Jews called *pogroms*.

In response a political movement known as Zionism began to campaign for a Jewish homeland in what was then called Palestine. However, Palestine at this time was already home to 400,000 Arabs.

Zionists chose several methods to achieve their aims. Some lobbied politicians, others founded farming communities in Palestine, and a few even launched terrorist attacks in the region to drive out non-Jewish people. Donations from across the world paid for Jewish people to return to Palestine in large numbers in the 1920s and 1930s.

racist policies. Other European countries did not welcome Jewish refugees, so many Jews fled to Palestine. Between 1922 and 1936, some 300,000 Jews arrived there. Some formed organizations that used violent tactics to drive Arabs and the British from what they claimed as their land.

During World War II (1939–1945), the Nazis killed six million Jews and other victims in the Holocaust (*Shoa* in Hebrew). But the British stopped Jewish survivors heading for Palestine. They were concerned that the territory was getting crowded and hard to control.

The Birth of Israel

After the war, many countries agreed that the Jews needed land. The United Nations (UN) proposed dividing Palestine into two countries, an Arab state consisting of 43 percent of the land and a Jewish state consisting of the rest. (Jerusalem and Bethlehem were to be separate self-governing cities.) The Arabs rejected the plan, arguing that the land was all theirs.

In the months before the British Army was due to leave Palestine in 1948, Jewish and Arab fighters attacked each others' communities. Jewish forces got the upper hand. They destroyed Arab villages to make

way for Jewish settlements. On May 14, 1948, the Zionist leader David Ben-Gurion declared the birth of the State of Israel. Arabs call this event *al-Nakba*—"the Catastrophe."

The Arab neighbors of the new state—Egypt, Jordan, Lebanon, Syria, and Iraq—invaded at once but were driven back. About 700,000 Arabs had to leave Israel. Some fled

▲ Arab women and children flee from their village after it was taken over by Israeli forces in June 1948.

to the West Bank, a hilly area west of the Jordan River. In 1949 Israel signed treaties that established its borders with its neighbors. It now controlled 75 percent of Palestine—more than the UN had

A WAR IN A WEEK

In the 1960s, Israel's worst enemy was Egyptian leader Gamal Abdul Nasser. He regularly threatened to invade Israel, mainly because such threats made him popular at home. Nasser strengthened his army and signed a pact with Syria and Jordan. In May 1967 the Egyptian army assembled in the Sinai Desert. Nasser probably had no real plans to invade— but Israel did not wait to find out.

Before dawn on June 5, Israeli bombers destroyed Egypt's entire air force in less than three hours. Next the Israeli planes attacked the aircraft of Jordan and Syria. Now that Israel was in complete control of the skies, its army was able to move into Egypt's Sinai, the

▲ Israeli troops celebrate in front of the Dome of the Rock on Temple Mount after capturing East Jerusalem from Jordan in June 1967.

West Bank area of Jordan, and the Golan Heights in Syria and Lebanon. By June 8, Israel controlled all these territories. The war was over by June 10, when the United Nations called for a ceasefire. Israel was left in control of the occupied areas. It had increased its territory through warfare for the second time.

JEWISH DIASPORA

One in every three Israeli Jews were born abroad. Their ancestors had been spread around the world, especially North Africa, the Middle East, and Europe, through the Diaspora. This is the name given to the long process by which Jews were forced out of Palestine. It began in the 8th century B.C. when the Jews were enslaved by the Babylonians. The dispersal of Jews reached new heights as the Romans crushed several rebellions, and it continued into the Middle Ages.

▲ Orthodox Jews in Jerusalem wear a style of clothing from 18th-century Eastern Europe.

proposed. The Gaza Strip became Egyptian, while Jordan took East Jerusalem, including the holy Temple Mount, and the West Bank.

From War to War

In 1950, the Israeli parliament passed the Law of Return. It gave all of the world's Jews the right to live in Israel. However, Israel continued to clash with its neighbors. In 1956, Egypt took control of the Suez Canal and blocked ships from reaching Israeli ports. In response Israel, Britain, and France attacked Egypt.

In 1967, after the Six Day War, Israel took control of Arab areas of Palestine: the West Bank, Gaza Strip, Sinai, and the Golan Heights. The areas became known as the Occupied Territories. About 500,000 Arabs lost their homes and fled to Jordan, Syria, and

Lebanon. The UN ordered Israel to withdraw, but it refused. The occupied land included the Western Wall, the most sacred place in Judaism. Religious Israelis began to build settlements in the Occupied Territories. They claimed that these regions lay within the borders of ancient Israel and had been promised to the Jews by God.

In 1973, Egypt and Syria attacked Israel on the Jewish holiday of Yom Kippur to try to get their land back. Israel, supported by the United States, again proved stronger. Under a 1979 treaty, Israel returned Sinai to Egypt. The other Occupied Territories remained under Israeli control.

Uprisings and Terror

Israel now came under attack from the Palestine Liberation Organization (PLO). This terrorist group attacked Israelis from its bases in southern Lebanon. From 1982 to 2000, Israeli forces occupied southern Lebanon, but they never entirely halted PLO terrorism.

In 1987 an uprising called the *Intifada* began in the Gaza Strip and the West Bank. Palestinians launched a violent campaign against Israeli troops, ranging from throwing stones to shooting and bombing.

In 1993, U.S. President Bill Clinton oversaw a deal between the two sides, known as the Oslo Accords. The Palestinians were given some control of the Occupied Territories in return for stopping attacks on Israel. The accords did not resolve whether Palestinians could return to their homes in Israel, however, or who would control Jerusalem. Meanwhile, Jewish settlers were still allowed to stay in the Occupied Territories.

After further peace talks collapsed in 2000, Palestinian terrorists launched a campaign of suicide bombings inside Israel. The Israeli government sent troops back into the West Bank. In 2003, another plan for peace was agreed on. This so-called Road Map required both sides to compromise. The Israeli government forced Jewish settlers to leave the Gaza Strip and parts of the West Bank. Some Israelis felt betrayed by the withdrawal. Others felt that it was the only way to make Israel safe and secure. On both sides, many people hoped that a new era had begun.

▼ Israeli police prepare to evict a Jewish family from its home in the Gaza Strip in August 2005. Despite protests from the settlers and other Israelis, the government saw the withdrawal as a necessary concession to the peace process.

Shalom Israel!

WHEN EARLY ISRAELI leaders welcomed Jewish immigrants from all over the world, they had to decide on a common language. They chose Hebrew. Hebrew was the language of the Bible, but few people had spoken it for thousands of years. When it became one of Israel's official languages, new words had to be invented for many everyday things, such as bicycles and ice cream. Hebrew is not easy to learn. It has its own alphabet and is written from right to left. People moving to Israel have to take intensive Hebrew lessons every day for five months to help them to settle in. Arabic is also an official language, and many Israelis speak English and other languages, too. Street signs often point the way in Hebrew, Arabic, and English.

◀ Boys with the traditional hair ringlets of Orthodox Jews read during a Hebrew lesson at a school in Zefat, a city in Galilee.

URBAN AND RURAL POPULATION

About 90 percent of Israelis live in towns or cities, usually in apartments. The capital, Jerusalem, is home to at least 700,000 people. Tel Aviv is the commercial and financial heart of Israel, and is one of the world's most expensive cities.

Many Israeli towns started as farming villages. Others are called "development towns" and were built during Israel's early years to house its growing population.

There are more than one million Arabs (Muslims and Christians) in Israel. Over half live in small towns and farm villages in the north of the country.

▶ One hundred years ago, Tel Aviv was an empty beach. Today it is Israel's second largest city.

Common Hebrew Phrases

Here are a few Hebrew words and phrases you might use in Israel. Give them a try:

Hello/Goodbye	Shalom (shah-LOM)
Please	Bevakasha (beh-va-ka-SHAH)
Thank you	Toda (to-DA)
You're welcome	Al lo davar (al-low dah-VAR)
Have a good Sabbath	Shabbat Shalom (shah-BAT shah-LOM)
Well done	Kol hakavod (KOL ha-ka-VOD)
What's your name? to male/female	Ma shimcha (ma shim-CHA)/Ma shmech (ma SHMECH)

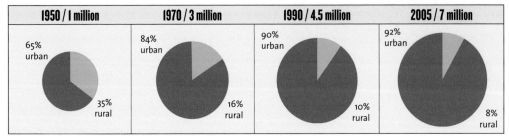

1950 / 1 million	1970 / 3 million	1990 / 4.5 million	2005 / 7 million
65% urban / 35% rural	84% urban / 16% rural	90% urban / 10% rural	92% urban / 8% rural

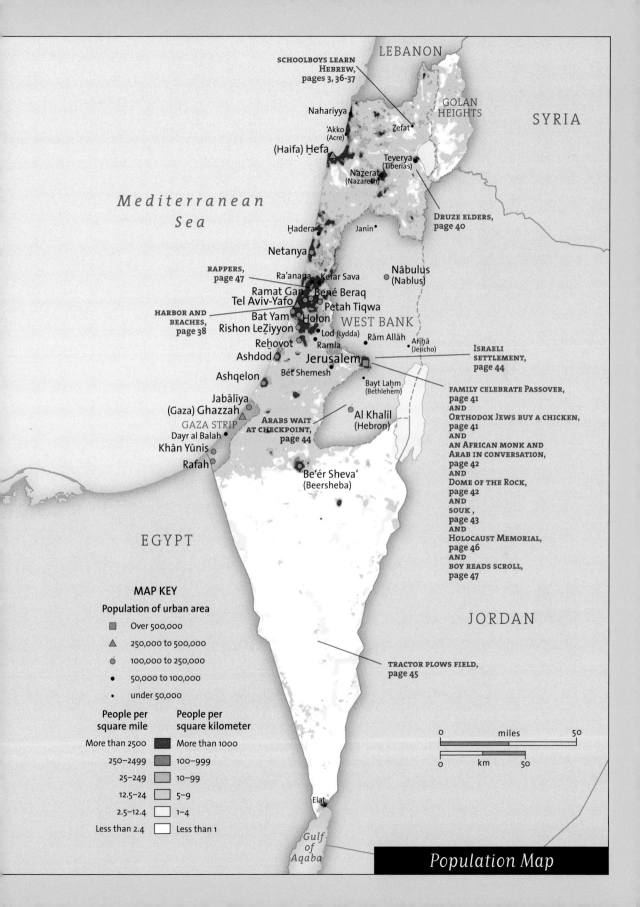

LEBANON

SCHOOLBOYS LEARN
HEBREW,
pages 3, 36-37

GOLAN
HEIGHTS

SYRIA

Nahariyya

'Akko
(Acre)

Zefat

(Haifa) Ḥefa

Teverya
(Tiberias)

Naẓerat
(Nazareth)

*Mediterranean
Sea*

DRUZE ELDERS,
page 40

Hadera

Janin

Netanya

Nābulus
(Nablus)

RAPPERS,
page 47

Ra'anana

Kefar Sava

Ramat Gan

Bené Beraq

Tel Aviv-Yafo

Petaḥ Tiqwa

HARBOR AND
BEACHES,
page 38

Bat Yam

Ḥolon

WEST BANK

Rishon LeẒiyyon

Lod (Lydda)

Reḥovot

Ramla

Rām Allāh

Arīḥā
(Jericho)

Ashdod

Jerusalem

ISRAELI
SETTLEMENT,
page 44

Bét Shemesh

FAMILY CELEBRATE PASSOVER,
page 41
AND
ORTHODOX JEWS BUY A CHICKEN,
page 41
AND
AN AFRICAN MONK AND
ARAB IN CONVERSATION,
page 42
AND
DOME OF THE ROCK,
page 42
AND
SOUK ,
page 43
AND
HOLOCAUST MEMORIAL,
page 46
AND
BOY READS SCROLL,
page 47

Ashqelon

Bayt Laḥm
(Bethlehem)

Jabālīya

(Gaza) Ghazzah

GAZA STRIP

Dayr al Balaḥ

ARABS WAIT
AT CHECKPOINT,
page 44

Al Khalīl
(Hebron)

Khān Yūnis

Rafah

Be'ér Sheva'
(Beersheba)

EGYPT

JORDAN

TRACTOR PLOWS FIELD,
page 45

MAP KEY

Population of urban area

◼	Over 500,000
▲	250,000 to 500,000
⬤	100,000 to 250,000
●	50,000 to 100,000
•	under 50,000

People per square mile	People per square kilometer
More than 2500	More than 1000
250–2499	100–999
25–249	10–99
12.5–24	5–9
2.5–12.4	1–4
Less than 2.4	Less than 1

miles
0   50

km
0   50

Elat

*Gulf
of
Aqaba*

Population Map

International Origins

It is impossible to describe a typical Israeli. About two-thirds of the population was born in Israel. The others have come from more than 100 different countries. Some Israeli Jews, known as Haredim, are highly religious and wear traditional clothing. Most Israeli Jews are not religious. They dress and live in a similar way to western Europeans or North Americans.

Many Israeli Jews are known according to where they originated. Ashkenazi Jews came from Central and Eastern Europe, Sephardic Jews, or Mizrahim, are largely from North Africa and across the rest of the Middle East.

New Arrivals

Israel offers a home to all Jews. When famine struck Ethiopia in 1985, the Israeli government allowed

A HOME TO MANY

About 20 percent of Israel's population are Arabs, whose families stayed in 1948. There are also about three million Arabs living in the Occupied Territories, areas that Israel took from Arab neighbors during the 1967 war. They are known as Palestinians. Most Palestinians are Muslims, although 100,000 of them are Christians.

Other communities make up a final 5 percent of Israel's people. The Druze speak Arabic and follow a secretive religion that is similar to Islam. Around 4,000 people are Circassians, non-Arabic Muslims. Finally, there are just 700 Samaritans. They consider themselves both Israeli and Palestinian, speaking Arabic but praying in Hebrew.

▲ Druze elders at the Tomb of Jethro, a sacred Druze shrine in northern Israel

REMEMBERING THE PAST

Religious festivals play a big role in Israeli life. Often they recall important events in Jewish history. One of the most important is Passover, celebrating the escape from slavery in Egypt thousands of years ago. Families eat flat bread, recalling how the Israelites did not have time to leave their bread to rise before beginning the journey.

Yom Kippur, one of the holiest days, is a somber event. Jews fast and pray for forgiveness. The country comes to a total halt—there is no public transportation and there is no radio or television.

▲ Children act out the story of Moses for their family before the Passover dinner.

At 11 o'clock on Holocaust Memorial Day sirens sound across the country. For two minutes everything stops as Israelis remember the dead.

30,000 Ethiopian Jews to settle in the country. There are now 120,000 Ethiopians in Israel. There are also 3,000 African Hebrew Israelites. These African Americans believe they are descendants of Jewish tribes that disappeared after the invasion by Assyria 2,700 years ago. In the 1990s, about 900,000 Russians moved to Israel after the collapse of the Soviet Union.

A steady stream of settlers also arrives in Israel from rich countries like France, Britain, and the United States. They want to live in a Jewish state, even though life there is sometimes tougher than they are used to.

▼ Orthodox Jews buy a chicken for Yom Kippur. In a cermony called *kapparot*, they will transfer their sins to the chicken.

▲ A monk from the Ethiopian Church talks to a Christian Arab on the roof of the Church of the Holy Sepulcher in Jerusalem.

A Day Off

At dusk on Friday, traditional Jewish families have a candlelit meal to begin Shabbat, the day of rest, which runs until Saturday evening. For most people, Shabbat is a chance to take a break, but religious families are careful to avoid all work. In some areas, strict Jews put up barriers to make sure no one drives. Elevators are programmed to stop on every floor so that no one has to "work" by pressing the buttons.

In the modern cities like Elat and Tel Aviv, many people do not observe Shabbat and businesses

A WALL AND A DOME

Both the Israelis and Palestinians regard Jerusalem as their capital. The clash is focused on a small hill in the east of the Holy City. Jews know it as Temple Mount. They stuff papers containing prayers into cracks in the last remaining wall of the temple. To Muslims, the hill is the Noble Sanctuary, the location of the Dome of the Rock. Access to the shrines is heavily controlled. Israel took control in 1967. Orthodox Jews say the land is theirs alone, while religious Muslims maintain that their important shrine must not be in non-Muslim hands.

▲ The Dome of the Rock houses a rock from which Prophet Muhammad is believed to have risen to heaven and met God.

remain open. However, when some stores opened on Shabbat to sell a new *Harry Potter* novel, the government fined them.

Religious Rules

The Jewish faith has more than 600 rules covering daily life. They are recorded in the Torah, the Jewish holy book. About 20 percent of Israelis try to follow the rules very closely. Most follow some, as they consider this part of being Jewish.

One rule some Israelis follow is only to eat food that is considered kosher, or acceptable in religious law. Kosher food has to be prepared in a certain way and excludes some meat and fish, such as pork or shellfish. Meat and dairy products cannot be mixed. That means no cheeseburgers or pizzas with pepperoni and cheese.

Busy streets in Israel are full of the tempting smells of food being cooked. The food reflects the many places Israelis have come from. Some favorite street food is Arabic in origin, such as *hummus* (mashed chickpeas) and delicious *falafel* (fried chickpea balls), which are eaten in flat breads called *pitas*. *Blintzes*, small rolled pastries filled with cheese, are similar to Russian pancakes—*blinis*—or Turkish *gözleme*.

▲ Shoppers buy vegetables and cooking equipment in one of Jerusalem's covered markets, or *souks*. This narrow street marks the boundary between the Christian and Muslim quarters of the Old City. There are also Jewish and Armenian quarters.

▲ Jewish settlements in the Occupied Territories, like this one in the West Bank, are usually built on high ground so that they are easier to defend.

▼ A Palestinian family waits to pass through an Israeli army checkpoint.

Keeping Their Distance

After years of fighting, Jewish Israelis rarely meet Palestinian Arabs living in the Occupied Territories. Nevertheless, if they were to share a meal they would find many things in common. For example, Muslims have similar food rules as Jews, including no pork.

Hospitality is important to Arabs, and visits have a special etiquette. Cold drinks are served first, followed by fruit, tea, and cakes. When coffee is served, it is time for visitors to leave.

However, other aspects of life in the Occupied Territories are very different from life in Israel itself. The Israelis living in settlements in the territories do not mix with their Arab neighbors. The settlements are considered illegal by most foreign countries, and they have been attacked by Palestinians. In Hebron, where Israelis and Palestinians live close together near the Tomb of Abraham, youths from both sides throw stones at one another. The Israeli communities have their own stores and restaurants, and live in apartment buildings on hillsides. These have bomb shelters in case of attack.

KIBBUTZ

In 1909 some Jewish settlers in Palestine set up the first *kibbutz*, meaning "collective." In this farming homestead, no one received payment—instead members received food and housing in return for their labor. The movement quickly spread and helped boost the development of Israel's economy in the 1950s. Communal living, hard work, and equality were very important. Everyone shared the tough jobs. Adults had private living quarters, but children were raised in a group. Today, Israel has over 250 kibbutzim, home to 100,000 members. Many are run as companies and have factories as well as farms. Children now grow up with their parents, but high-schoolers are expected to work in the kibbutz a day a week.

▲ A tractor plows a kibbutz farm in the Negev.

The settlements have their own roads into Israel. Arabs are not allowed to use them. Arabs must travel along routes guarded by checkpoints of Israeli soldiers.

Outdoor Fun

Jewish Israeli children like to do similar things to Americans of the same age: They play computer

NATIONAL HOLIDAYS

Most of Israel's public holidays celebrate Jewish festivals or commemorate the foundation of Israel. They are held according to the Hebrew year, which is 11 days shorter than the Western calendar. As a result holidays fall on different dates from year to year.

SEPTEMBER–OCTOBER	Rosh Hashanah (New Year), Yom Kippur, Sukkot
NOVEMBER–DECEMBER	Hanukkah
FEBRUARY–MARCH	Purim (Feast of Esther)
MARCH–APRIL	Pesach (Passover)
APRIL–MAY	Holocaust Memorial Day Independence Day
MAY–JUNE	Shavuot (Harvest festival)
JULY–AUGUST	Tish'a Be-Av (Commemorates the destruction of the First and Second Temples)

▲ The Holocaust Memorial in Jerusalem is a huge underground maze.

games, go to the beach, or play basketball, judo, or other sports. Because Israel has a warm climate, children often play outside. At the beach they play *matkot*, a game using wooden paddles and a small ball. Most matkot games are not competitive: Players try to hit the ball to one another in long rallies. Palestinian children enjoy playing soccer in the street. In general, they have less access to leisure facilities than children in Israel. Most Arab children living in the West Bank have never seen the beach, even though it is just a few miles away.

Time to Grow Up

At age 13, Jewish boys celebrate their bar mitzvah. It is an important stage of growing up. In the eyes of the Jewish faith, it means they are now old enough to make their own religious decisions, rather than accept their parents'. The girls' version of the celebration is called a bat mitzvah and is celebrated at age 12. The boys and girls read at synagogue, the Jewish place of prayer. Afterward, there is a party.

Most Israeli teenagers are allowed to mix with both boys and girls and go on dates. Palestinian teenagers are not supposed to mix. When they are older, their parents have an important say about whom they marry.

Haredim Jews also live in segregated communities, where boys and girls do not mix. They have arranged marriages. A matchmaker called a *shadachan* introduces couples, and accepts a fee if the match is successful.

▲ A young boy reads from the Torah during his bar mitzvah at the Western Wall in Jerusalem.

Words and Songs

Israelis are great readers. Israeli writers publish a huge number of books in Hebrew, Arabic, and English. One of the most famous Israeli writers is Amos Oz, who tells stories about life in modern Israel and coping with the frequent violence.

Among the most interesting Israeli bands are the rappers DAM. Their name means "blood" in both Arabic and Hebrew. DAM are Arab Israelis who rap about not being fully part of either of Israel's communities: They are neither true Israelis nor Palestinian.

◀ Rappers from the Israeli hip-hop group Subliminal perform in central Israel. Their songs are about what it is like growing up in Israel.

An Armed Nation

SOLDIERS ARE EVERYWHERE in Israel. They are a reminder that peace is fragile. In settlements in the Occupied Territories, teachers and students carry guns to class. Even in cities like Tel Aviv, teenagers stroll around with submachine guns on their shoulders. They are off-duty members of the Israel Defense Forces (IDF). They carry their weapons to avoid any chance that they will be stolen and fall into the hands of terrorists. Most Jewish Israelis join the IDF after school. Men serve for three years, and women for two. Most Arab Israelis are not enlisted.

Recruits are sworn in at the Western Wall. Special forces units hold ceremonies at Masada, where Jewish rebels held out against the Romans 2,000 years ago. The troops vow that "Masada shall not fall again."

◄ **Students at a high school in a Jewish settlement in the West Bank put their guns under their desks before class.**

ISRAELI POLITICS

The conflict between Israel, the Palestinians, and other Arab nations dominates politics in Israel. Ehud Olmert, the current prime minister, is the leader of the Kadima (Forward) party. This party was founded in 2005. Its most important policy is returning parts of the Occupied Territories to Palestinian control. When the party came to power in 2006, it invited the left-wing Ha-Avoda (Labor) party to join it in government.

Currently, the third most popular party is Likud. Likud has conservative policies and opposes an Israeli withdrawal from the Occupied Territories. The extremist Ichud Leumi (National Union) party is popular with Jewish settlers in the Occupied Territories. It would like to see the Arabs leave these areas.

▶ The moon rises above the Knesset, Israel's parliament building in Jerusalem. The Knesset has 120 members, like the ancient Jewish assembly in biblical times.

Trading Partners

Most of Israel's neighbors have trade bans in place against the country. As a result, few goods pass across Israel's land borders, which are heavily guarded and slow to cross. Most of Israel's trade is with North America and Europe, with goods leaving and arriving by sea through ports such as Haifa. Israel's major exports are food, electronic equipment, high-tech engineering parts, and cut diamonds. The country imports fuel, cars, rough (uncut) diamonds, and machinery.

Country	Percent Israel exports
United States	36.7%
Belgium	7.5%
Hong Kong (China)	4.9%
United Kingdom	3.7%
All others combined	47.2%

Country	Percent Israel imports
United States	14.9%
Belgium	10.1%
Germany	7.5%
Switzerland	6.5%
United Kingdom	6.1%
All others combined	54.9%

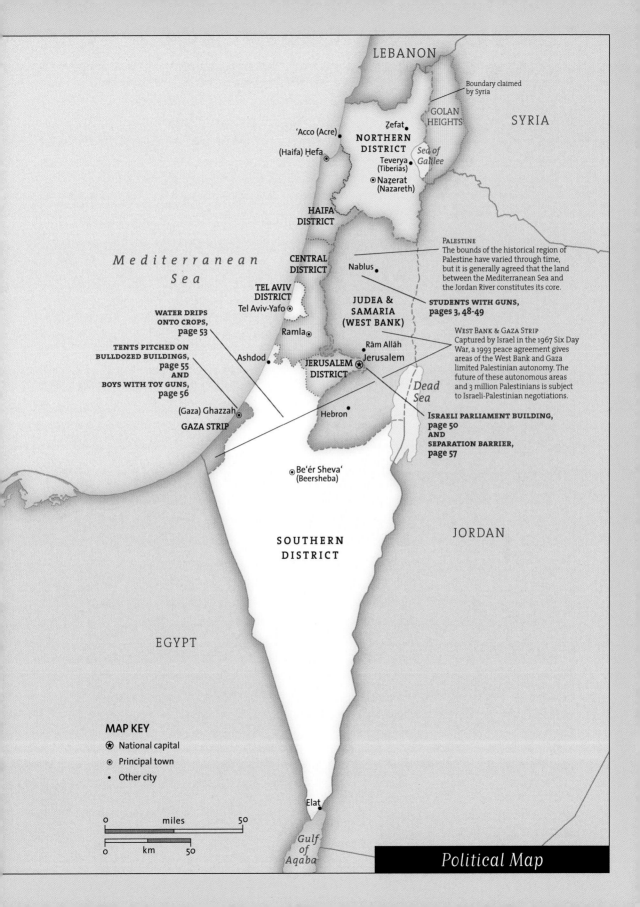

LEBANON

Boundary claimed
by Syria

GOLAN
HEIGHTS

SYRIA

Ẓefat

NORTHERN
DISTRICT

'Acco (Acre)

(Haifa) Ḥefa

*Sea of
Galilee*

Teverya
(Tiberias)

◉Naẓerat
(Nazareth)

HAIFA
DISTRICT

*M e d i t e r r a n e a n
S e a*

CENTRAL
DISTRICT

Nablus

PALESTINE
The bounds of the historical region of
Palestine have varied through time,
but it is generally agreed that the land
between the Mediterranean Sea and
the Jordan River constitutes its core.

TEL AVIV
DISTRICT

Tel Aviv-Yafo ◉

JUDEA &
SAMARIA
(WEST BANK)

STUDENTS WITH GUNS,
pages 3, 48-49

WATER DRIPS
ONTO CROPS,
page 53

Ramla ◉

WEST BANK & GAZA STRIP
Captured by Israel in the 1967 Six Day
War, a 1993 peace agreement gives
areas of the West Bank and Gaza
limited Palestinian autonomy. The
future of these autonomous areas
and 3 million Palestinians is subject
to Israeli-Palestinian negotiations.

TENTS PITCHED ON
BULLDOZED BUILDINGS,
page 55
AND
BOYS WITH TOY GUNS,
page 56

Rām Allāh

Ashdod

Jerusalem

JERUSALEM
DISTRICT ✪

*Dead
Sea*

(Gaza) Ghazzah ◉

Hebron

ISRAELI PARLIAMENT BUILDING,
page 50
AND
SEPARATION BARRIER,
page 57

GAZA STRIP

Be'ér Sheva'
(Beersheba)

SOUTHERN
DISTRICT

JORDAN

EGYPT

MAP KEY

✪ National capital

◉ Principal town

• Other city

Elat

0   miles   50

0   km   50

*Gulf
of
Aqaba*

Political Map

Learning to Live Alone

Israel has come a long way since its foundation in 1948, when it was largely a nation of farming communities. Israelis study and work hard. After serving in the IDF, half of all Israelis go to college to continue their education.

Israelis are no longer mainly farmers. Ten percent of Israelis now work for one of about 4,000 technology companies in the country. Israelis have a reputation for being innovative and self-sufficient. Surrounded by hostile neighbors, they have learned to make the most of their own resources.

HOW THE GOVERNMENT WORKS

Israel is the only fully democratic country in the Middle East. Elections are held every four years to select members of the parliament, or Knesset. Any party that wins more than 2 percent of the votes is entitled to seats, so the Knesset normally contains members from a number of parties, none of which has overall control. That means that parties must join together in coalitions to form governments. The leader of the largest party normally becomes prime minister. The prime minister appoints a cabinet (team of ministers) to run the country. While the prime minister runs the country, Israel's head of state is the president. The president is elected by members of the Knesset. He or she swears in the Supreme Court judges. Religious courts for each of Israel's main religions work alongside Israel's district courts.

GOVERNMENT		
EXECUTIVE	LEGISLATIVE	JUDICIARY
PRIME MINISTER	KNESSET (120 MEMBERS)	SUPREME COURT
CABINET	REGIONAL COUNCILS	DISTRICT COURTS

One area of technology in which Israel is a world leader is water conservation. Water is so precious that scientists have developed the latest irrigation techniques. They use computers to drip just the right amount of water onto crops so not a drop is wasted. The technology behind instant messaging and voice mail was also invented in Israel.

As well as being a high-tech manufacturer, Israel is also a financial center. It is home to one of the world's biggest diamond exchanges, where the precious stones are bought and sold.

▲ This pill developed in Israel contains a camera that records a video as it passes through the body.

Paying the Cost

Israel's need to be constantly ready to defend itself is expensive—and not just financially. Some Israelis worry that drafting young people into the IDF makes them less sensitive and more hostile toward the Palestinians. The IDF also costs a lot of money. A short war in Lebanon in 2006, for example, cost Israel more than $1 billion. The Israeli economy is generally strong but even so the high costs of

▼ Water drips onto a seedling in a high-tech irrigation system developed in Israel.

AGRICULTURE MAP

Israel's early economy was based on farming as settlers toiled to produce enough food to support the country. Today, all suitable land is covered with fields, greenhouses, and orchards. In recent times, the economy has become more high tech, with factories making communications equipment and precision engineering tools.

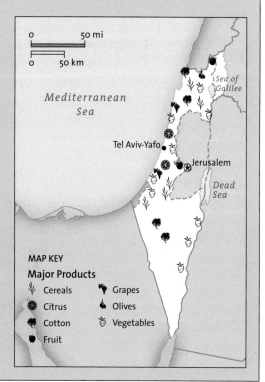

0   50 mi

0   50 km

Mediterranean Sea

Sea of Galilee

Tel Aviv-Yafo

Jerusalem

Dead Sea

MAP KEY
Major Products
Cereals		Grapes
Citrus		Olives
Cotton		Vegetables
Fruit		

defense are paid at the expense of other things, such as free universities.

Another cost of the fragile peace is the loss of tourism. Israel once drew many visitors, particularly to its holy sites. Now many foreigners consider it too dangerous to visit. Fewer tourists come—and bring less money into the Israeli economy. About 9 percent of Israelis are unemployed. With so many immigrants arriving in the country, even highly skilled workers can find it difficult to get a job.

Powerful Friends

The Israeli economy depends on money from Israel's main ally, the United States. Since 1948, the United States has given Israel more than $84 billion in aid. The United States wants to make sure that Israel remains stable in the troubled Middle East. (The United States pays a similar amount to Egypt and a smaller sum to Jordan for the same reason.) Germany continues to give $500 million a year to Israel in compensation for the Holocaust. Israel also receives financial donations from individuals and organizations around the world.

▲ President Bill Clinton looks on as Yitzhak Rabin shakes hands with Yasser Arafat, the PLO leader, after signing the Oslo Accords peace agreement in 1993.

Palestinian Divisions

Since 1994, part of the Occupied Territories has been governed by the Palestinian National Authority. Its president, Mahmoud Abbas, leads the political group Fatah, which has decided to work peacefully with Israel. It aims to unite land the Arabs lost in 1967—the Gaza Strip and the West Bank—under a Palestinian

▼ Palestinians live in a tent village on the site of destroyed buildings in Gaza City. The buildings were bulldozed by the Israeli army, which said they were being used by Palestinian snipers.

government. Some Palestinians have turned to a group with different aims and methods. Hamas wants to destroy Israel and reclaim all the Arab land lost in 1948. It is prepared to use violence to achieve its aims. Hamas is popular with some poor Palestinians because it provides basic things like schools and hospitals.

In 2006, Hamas won Palestinian elections and took control of the government. Because of Hamas's links to terrorism, most countries stopped giving financial aid to the Palestinians. The Occupied Territories became increasingly chaotic. In 2007, Hamas gunmen seized control of the Gaza Strip, and amid the crisis Abbas dismissed the Hamas government.

Behind the Wall

As part of its plan to eventually withdraw from the Occupied Territories, in 2003 Israel began to build a

TROUBLE IN GAZA

Israel's 2005 decision to abandon settlements in the Gaza Strip won support both inside and outside the country. But critics complain that the withdrawal did not bring stability. The rival Palestinian groups, Fatah and Hamas, fought for control. Although Hamas won in Gaza, Fatah remains in power in the West Bank. Hamas now fire missiles into Israel from the Gaza Strip. The Israelis control movement in and out of the territories because of the terrorist threat. Gaza's economy has collapsed because none of its exports are allowed out. Three-quarters of its factories

▲ Boys with toy guns crawl along the ground at a Hamas rally in Gaza in 2006. Hamas makes great efforts to recruit young Palestinians.

have shut down. Some observers are concerned that poverty will lead more young Palestinians to turn to extreme ways to achieve political power, such as terrorism.

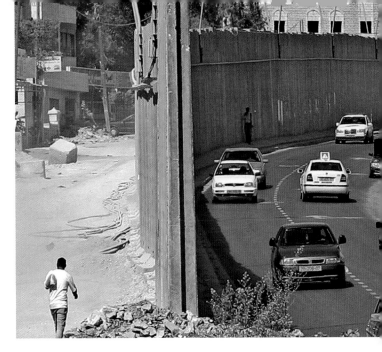

security barrier several hundred miles long around the West Bank. The government says that the wall will stop suicide bombers from entering Israel. Palestinians protest that the wall cuts towns and farms in half and encloses land that does not belong to Israel. Some people say the wall will turn the West Bank into a prison. The Israelis say the wall will come down when things are more peaceful.

▲ Israelis drive past a concrete barrier that separates them from the West Bank Palestinian town on the other side. Much of the barrier follows Israel's 1967 borders, although Palestinians complain that it also claims land for Israel that lay outside those borders.

The Path to Peace

Peace between the Palestinians and Israelis would not just improve the lives of both groups. It might also help bring stability to the whole Middle East. Problems remain, however. Four million Palestinians live abroad, mainly in refugee camps. They want to return to their former homes. If the Palestinians are allowed to return, however, Israeli Jews worry that they would soon be outnumbered. In terms of population numbers alone, Israel would no longer be a Jewish state.

Such obstacles often make peace in Israel seem far away. But at the same time, some ordinary Israelis and Palestinians try to put their differences aside. As long as people on both sides realize that they have to try to live together, there is hope for the future.

Add a Little Extra to Your Country Report!

I f you are assigned to write a report about Israel, you'll want to include basic information about the country, of course. The Fast Facts chart on page 8 will give you a good start. The rest of the book will give you the details you need to create a full and up-to-date paper or PowerPoint presentation. But what can you do to make your report more fun than anyone else's? If you use your imagination and dig a bit deeper into some of the topics introduced in this book, you're sure to come up with information that will make your report unique!

>Flag

Perhaps you could explain the history of Israel's flag, and the meanings of its colors and symbol. Go to **www.crwflags.com/fotw/flags** for more information.

>National Anthem

How about downloading Israel's national anthem, and playing it for your class? At **www.nationalanthems.info** you'll find what you need, including the words to the anthem, plus sheet music for it. Simply pick "I" and then "Israel" from the list on the left-hand side of the screen, and you're on your way.

>Time Difference

If you want to understand the time difference between Israel and where you are, this Web site can help: **www.worldtimeserver.com**. Just pick "Israel" from the list on the left. If you called someone in Israel right now, would you wake them up from their sleep?

>Currency

Another Web site will convert your money into shekels, the currency used in Israel.
You'll want to know how much money to bring if you're ever lucky enough to travel to Israel: **www.xe.com/ucc**.

>Weather

Why not check the current weather in Israel? It's easy—go to **www.weather.com** to find out if it's sunny or cloudy, warm or cold in Israel right now! Pick "World" from the headings at the top of the page. Then search for Israel. Click on any city. Be sure to click on the tabs below the weather report for Sunrise/Sunset information, Weather Watch, and Business Travel Outlook, too. Scroll down the page for the 36-hour Forecast and a satellite weather map. Compare your weather to the weather in the Israeli city you chose. Is this a good season, weather-wise, for a person to travel to Israel?

>Miscellaneous

Still want more information? Simply go to National Geographic's World Atlas for Young Explorers at **http://www.nationalgeographic.com/kids-world.atlas/**. It will help you find maps, photos, music, games, and other features that you can use to jazz up your report.

Glossary

Aqueduct a raised channel that carries water across a valley. The Romans built many to supply their cities with water.

Circa about; used to indicate a date that is approximate, and abbreviated as ca.

Climate the average weather of a certain place at different times of year.

Conservative a way of thinking that prefers to keep, or conserve, things as they are. Some political parties are described as conservative. An alternative description is right wing.

Crusade a religious war fought against members of another religion.

Culture a collection of beliefs, traditions, and styles that belongs to people living in a certain part of the world.

Economy the system by which a country creates wealth through making and trading in products.

Ecosystem a community of living things and the environment they interact with; an ecosystem includes plants, animals, soil, water, and air.

Empire territories located in several parts of the world that are controlled by a single nation.

Exile when someone is forced to leave their home country and live abroad.

Exported transported and sold outside the country of origin.

Extremist a person or organization that holds a set of extreme ideas, which most people would not agree with.

Habitat a part of the environment that is suitable for certain plants and animals.

Hospitality the way that people welcome guests to their homes.

Imported brought into the country from abroad.

Innovative good at coming up with new ideas to solve problems.

Judaism the religion followed by Jews.

Left wing a political term used to describe ideas that put the welfare of many people ahead of the welfare of one person. Left-wing politicians want to make changes so their countries will become more equal for all.

Mineral a chemical that is found in rocks or water. Salt is a common mineral.

Plateau a flat area that is high up.

Scavenger a meat-eating animal that does not kill prey but eats the flesh of dead animals.

Shrine a place that is important to the follower of a religion. Most shrines are located at a tomb or on the site of an important historical event.

Sniper a hidden gunman who shoots at the enemy from a long way away.

Species a type of organism; animals or plants in the same species look similar and can only breed successfully among themselves.

Synagogue the building where Jewish people gather to worship.

Treaty an agreement between two or more countries.

United Nations (UN) an international organization that includes most of the countries of the world. The UN is where governments discuss the world's problems and figure out how to work together to solve them.

Bibliography

DuBois, Jill. *Israel*. New York, NY: Benchmark Books, 2004.

Goldstein, Margaret. *Israel in Pictures*. Minneapolis, MN: Lerner Publications Co., 2004.

Schroeder, Holly. *Israel ABCs: A Book About the People and Places of Israel*. Minneapolis, MN: Picture Window Books, 2004.

http://www.goisrael.com/tourism_eng
(general information about the country from the Israeli Ministry of Tourism)

http://www.knesset.gov.il
(official Web site of the Knesset, the Israeli parliament)

Further Information

NATIONAL GEOGRAPHIC Articles

Finkel, Michael. "Bethlehem 2007 A. D." NATIONAL GEOGRAPHIC (December 2007): 58–85.

Web sites to explore

More fast facts about Israel, from the CIA (Central Intelligence Agency):
https://www.cia.gov/library/publications/the-world-factbook/geos/is.html

Do you want to know more about the history and politics of Israel? Take a look at http://www.jewishvirtuallibrary.org/jsource/index

The story of David and Goliath is central to Jewish traditions and the ideas behind the state of Israel. Learn more about it and other important events

in early Jewish history at: http://www.historyforkids.org/learn/religion/jews/david.htm

Is there anything else you'd like to know about Israel? This kid-friendly site has many fun facts: http://www.akhlah.com/israel/israel.php

Take a look at what is happening in Israel right now with the webcams on this site: http://www.isracamera.co.il/

See, hear

There are many ways to get a taste of life in Israel, such as movies, music, magazines, or TV shows. You might be able to locate these:

The Zigzag Kid (1998)
This illustrated novel by David Grossman has been translated from Hebrew into English and

many other languages. It tells the story of twelve-year-old Amnon, or "Nonny," who is one week away from his bar mitzvah. He takes the train from Jerusalem heading to Haifa but ends up having an amazing adventure.

DAM
Listen to the Arab-Israeli rap crew at their Web site: http://www.dampalestine.com/

Ushpizin (2005)
Although they are often viewed as being serious people, this comedy shows that the Orthodox Jews have a funny side like anyone else. The film tells how the lives of a religious couple struggling to make ends meet in Jerusalem become entangled with a pair of convicts on the run. Watch some clips at: http://www.ushpizin.com/home.html

Index

Credits

Picture Credits

Front Cover – Spine: Michael Selivanov/Shutterstock; Top: Richard Nowtiz/NGIC; Low Far Left: James L. Stanfield/NGIC; Low Left: Annie Griffiths Belt/NGIC; Low Right: Nicole Duplaix/NGIC; Low Far Right: Annie Griffiths Belt/NGIC.

Interior – Corbis: Mahfouz Abu/Turk/Reuters: 57 up; Shawn Baldwin: 56 lo; Bettmann: 30 lo, 31 up, 32 up, 32 lo; Clive Druett/Papilio: 19 up; Shai Ginott: 12 up; Joe Hollander/epa: 3 right, 48-49; Ed Kashi: 44 lo; Steve Kaufman: 2 right, 14-15; Robert Mulder/Godong: 47 up; Richard T. Nowitz: 11 up, 41 up, 45 up; Eyal Ofer: 35 lo; Reuters: 53 up, 55 up; Patrick Robert/Sygma: 34 up; Ricki Rosen/Saba: 27 lo; David Rubinger: 13 up; Studio Eye: 10 lo; Micah Walter: 47 lo; Getty Images: Nathan Bilow/Allsport: TP; Uriel Sinai: 26 up; NGIC: Ira Block: 27 up; Robert Clark: 28 lo; Jodi Cobb: 43 up; 44 up; David Doubilet: 19 lo; Nicole Duplaix: 20 lo; Kenneth Garrett: 18 up, 24 up; Martin Gray: 42 lo; Annie Griffiths Belt: 3 left, 20 up, 33 up, 36-37, 42 up, 46 lo; Richard Nowitz: 2 left, 6-7, 11 lo, 28 up, 29 up, 50 lo; Reza: 55 lo; James L. Stanfield: 2-3, 5 up, 13 lo, 21 lo, 22-23, 38 lo, 41 lo, 53 lo; B. Anthony Stewart: 40 lo; Roy Toft: 16 lo; Priit Vesilind: 10 up; Shutterstock: Pavel Bernshtarn: 59 up.

Text copyright © 2008 National Geographic Society
Published by the National Geographic Society.
All rights reserved. Reproduction of the whole or any part of the contents without written permission from the National Geographic Society is strictly prohibited.

For information about special discounts for bulk purchases, contact National Geographic Special Sales: ngspecsales@ngs.org

For more information, please call 1-800-NGS-LINE (647-5463) or write to the following address:

NATIONAL GEOGRAPHIC SOCIETY
1145 17th Street N.W.
Washington, D.C. 20036-4688 U.S.A.

Visit us online at www.nationalgeographic.com/books

Library of Congress Cataloging-in-Publication Data available on request
ISBN: 978-1-4263-0258-9

Printed in the United States of America

11/WOR/3

Series design by Jim Hiscott.
The body text is set in Avenir; Knockout.
The display text is set in Matrix Script.

Front Cover—Top: A tourist sunbathes on a beach at the Dead Sea; Low Far Left: Close-up of a bride's hands; Low Left: Jerusalem, with the Dome of the Rock and the Church of the Holy Sepulcher; Low Right: Fennec fox; Low Far Right: An off-duty soldier and Orthodox Jews use telephones, Jerusalem.

Page 1—Boys play with a soccer ball in Jerusalem; Icon image on spine, Contents page, and throughout: Western Wall

Produced through the worldwide resources of the National Geographic Society

John M. Fahey, Jr., *President and Chief Executive Officer*; Gilbert M. Grosvenor, *Chairman of the Board*; Tim T. Kelly, *President, Global Media Group*; Nina D. Hoffman, *Executive Vice President, President of Book Publishing Group*

National Geographic Staff for this Book

Nancy Laties Feresten, *Vice President, Editor-in-Chief of Children's Books*
Bea Jackson, *Director of Design and Illustration*
Jim Hiscott, *Art Director*
Virginia Koeth, *Project Editor*
Lori Epstein, *Illustrations Editor*
Stacy Gold, Nadia Hughes, *Illustrations Research Editors*
R. Gary Colbert, *Production Director*
Lewis R. Bassford, *Production Manager*
Maryclare Tracy, Nicole Elliott, *Manufacturing Managers*
Maps, *Mapping Specialists, Ltd.*

Brown Reference Group plc. Staff for this Book

Volume Editor: Tom Jackson
Designer: Dave Allen
Picture Manager: Clare Newman
Maps: Martin Darlison
Artwork: Darren Awuah
Index: Kay Ollerenshaw
Senior Managing Editor: Tim Cooke
Children's Publisher: Anne O'Daly
Editorial Director: Lindsey Lowe

About the Author

EMMA YOUNG has worked in publishing for five years and also works in television production. She has written articles on a wide range of subjects, including history and science. Emma is married and lives in London.

About the Consultants

ZVI BEN-DOR BENITE is Associate Professor of History and Middle Eastern and Islamic Studies at New York University. Professor Ben-Dor Benite is the author of *The Dao of Muhammad: A Cultural History of Muslims in Late Imperial China* (Harvard 2005) and has published on Islamic, Chinese, Israeli, and Middle Eastern history.

GEORGE J. KANAZI is professor of Arabic literature at the University of Haifa, Israel. His research focuses on medieval Arabic literature, mainly poetry. Two of his books were published by the Academy of Arabic Language in Damascus, a very rare case of an Israeli scholar being published in Syria.

AVIVA HALAMISH is a professor of history at the Open University of Israel. Her research focuses on the history of the Jewish people and of Palestine in the twentieth century, with emphasis on immigration and on Arab-Jewish relations. She has recently completed a three-volume series entitled *From a National Home to a State in the Making: The Jewish Community in Palestine between the World Wars* (in Hebrew and Russian). Professor Halamish is vice-president of the Association for Israel Studies.